The
Gospel
Unplugged

The Gospel Unplugged

The Good News Plain and Simple

J.B. HIXSON

LUCIDBOOKS

DEDICATION

To Bethany, Brooke, Morgan, Landry, Faith, Abby

"Behold, children are a heritage from the Lord,
the fruit of the womb is a reward.
Like arrows in the hand of a warrior,
so are the children of one's youth.
Happy is the man who has his quiver full of them;
they shall not be ashamed,
but shall speak with their enemies in the gate."

(Psalm 127:3-5)

ACKNOWLEDGEMENTS

I wish to acknowledge the significant impact that the writings of Lewis Sperry Chafer have had on my theology. He was a true champion of grace, and you will notice several of his profound quotations throughout this book. If you read only one more book in your life and you have not yet read Chafer's *Salvation*, please put this book down and go read *Salvation*.

As always, I wish to thank my wife Wendy for her unwavering support and love through all of the ups and downs of ministry. I love you. You are wonderful.

Thank you, also, to Bethany, Brooke, Morgan, Landry, Faith and Abby who sacrifice time with their Dad so that I can be involved in ministry. I love you.

Thank you to my parents who taught me the simple Gospel message when I was a child and led me to faith in Christ. I love you.

I wish to thank Grace School of Theology for giving me the freedom to work on various writing projects while serving as an administrator and faculty member. It is an honor to serve in such a fine institution where the clear Gospel is advanced unashamedly. For more information about Grace School of Theology please visit www.gsot.org.

Thank you also to Logos Bible Software for their partnership—both formal and informal—over the last eleven years. Without this amazing software, it would simply be impossible for me to juggle my various ministry obligations and writing projects. Thank you, Logos, for this unparalleled tool for Bible study. For more information about Logos Bible Software, please visit www.logos.com

Many thanks to Linus Nguyen for his friendship, service and partnership in ministry.

I am especially thankful for the help of Travis Gasper in putting this book together.

O how unlike the complex works of man,
Heav'n's easy, artless, unencumber'd plan!
No meretricious graces to beguile,
No clustering ornaments to clog the pile;
From ostentation, as from weakness, free,
It stands like the cerulean arch we see,
Majestic in its own simplicity.
Inscribed above the portal, from afar
Conspicuous as the brightness of a star,
Legible only by the light they give,
Stand the soul-quickening words—
BELIEVE, AND LIVE.

(William Cowper, *Truth*)

CONTENTS

PREFACE

As I write this preface, events are unfolding in the geopolitical realm that have many experts worried about the future of our country. At the top of the list is the economic crisis. Our nation's debt has reached the tipping point. We are past the point of no return. It is only a matter of time before the U.S. dollar loses its privileged status as the world's reserve currency. Already, other first world nations are dropping the dollar as their means of exchange internationally.

The private Federal Reserve—that's right, the Federal Reserve is no more *Federal* than *Federal Express*—cannot keep printing money to cover our losses. Sooner or later the dollar will crash, and the global offshore banking cartel, which owns the Federal Reserve, will take our money and run, leaving America in a state of utter chaos. It is not just government or union pension plans that are being looted. Private retirement accounts are at risk as well. All of this is very bad news.

Add to the economic crisis the unrest in Northern Africa and throughout the Middle East—throughout the world really. Everywhere we turn, skirmishes are popping up. The tension between the United States and Pakistan is particularly unsettling. Many of our allies are making behind the scenes deals with other nations because they fear what is coming. Israel's status as a sovereign nation is being threatened more today than at any other time since 1948. Russia is not the dismantled former-Communist super power that most people think it is. China, despite economic woes of its own, is saber-rattling. Many experts warn we are spiraling toward World War III. This is bad news indeed.

Add to that the threat of isolated attacks throughout the world by smaller terrorist groups seeking to advance their cause.

Or rogue dictators using military force for ethnic cleansing. We see regular news reports of tragic bombings or attacks in other countries. Innocent civilians die every day at the hands of hostile sectarian groups. More bad news.

And then there are the black operations and contract mercenaries we never hear anything about. An entire underworld exists where unspeakable crimes are carried out every day. The sickening enterprise of human trafficking, including child sex rings, is a horrific, daily reality for thousands of victims throughout the world. The bad news seems to get worse and worse. It just keeps piling up.

If all of this isn't bad enough, we are witnessing the systematic dismantling of American freedom right before our eyes. The Bill of Rights—particularly the First, Second and Fourth Amendments—is becoming a thing of the past as a full-fledged police state is rolled out incrementally from coast to coast.

Warrantless checkpoints; gun confiscation drills; TSA groping; free speech zones; government controlled thermostats; biometric tracking on every street corner; license-plate readers; carbon taxes; government Fusion Centers; no-refusal blood warrants; a national passport program; black boxes in new automobiles; implantable RFID chips; radiation chambers; cell phone and computer monitoring; FEMA Camps; the Internet Takeover Bill (AKA Cyber Security Act); public schools spying on students via government-issued laptops. I don't mean to sound paranoid, but how can anyone *not* see these trends as bad news?

You might be wondering at this point, "Why in the world should I keep reading? All of this sounds so depressing." It's true....reality can be very depressing. With all of the bad news in the world today, people are searching for answers. Perhaps that is where you find yourself. It all seems so overwhelming. Where can you turn to find perspective and hope? Isn't there some *good news* in the middle of all of this bad news?

The answer is a resounding "Yes!" And that is why I wrote this book. I am going to present you with some amazing good news—good news that transcends everything else in life. It is a timeless truth with eternal ramifications revealed by the Creator Himself. It is called the *Gospel*.

The wonderful thing about the Gospel is that it is clear and simple. When everything else in life seems confusing or unpredictable, the Gospel speaks to your most paramount need. The Gospel is fundamental to all of life. And I'd like to introduce you to it in the pages that follow.

But first, let me give you another reason why I wrote this book. I am passionate about the Gospel for all of the reasons I just mentioned. It is what matters most in life. It provides the answer to all of life's problems. It addresses the most important aspect of humanity. But sadly, many people—even many churches and Christian leaders—have abandoned the plain and simple message of the Gospel. This troubles me. And I think a short book that reintroduces us to the clear good news of the Gospel is much needed today.

Vince Lombardi is widely recognized as one of the greatest football coaches of all time. On one occasion, after a particularly tough loss for his team, he gathered his players in the locker room for the usual postgame speech. In a short but poignant statement, the coach cut right to the heart of the matter. Holding up a football, Lombardi quipped, "Gentlemen, *this* is a football." Of course these professional football players all knew what a football was. But the coach's point was not lost on them: Their performance in the game that just concluded had evidenced an utter lack of competency in the most basic fundamentals of the game.

A survey of the state of Christianity in America reveals a similar incompetency when it comes to the basics of the Christian faith—namely, the Gospel. Somewhere along the way we seem to have lost sight of the most important aspect of Christianity. There is a crisis regarding the nature of the gospel within Christianity today and very little is being done to address the issue. While most Christians agree that Jesus Christ is the focus of the Gospel, there is widespread disagreement regarding the specific details of the Gospel.

The trend toward the abandonment of certainty, as well as a general disdain within contemporary culture for absolute truth, have created fertile ground for erroneous gospel messages—each competing for legitimacy within the Christian church at large.

Perhaps most disturbing is the fact that each of these inherently contradictory gospel messages is welcomed as a legitimate pretender to the true Gospel, and few, if any, Christian leaders seem concerned with this self-evident problem. This suggests at least a couple of possibilities. (1) Either Christian leaders simply are not paying attention to what other Christian leaders are saying about the gospel and thus have not noticed the problem; and/or (2) each Christian leader does not hold his or her particular view of the Gospel with any degree of conviction and thus is open to embracing competing views on the matter. Either explanation does not speak well of the state of Christianity today.

What is needed today is a Lombardi-style critique in which we confidently raise our Bibles and remind the world, "This is the Gospel!"

A growing trend among popular bands and singers is to record "unplugged" TV concerts. The huge arena is replaced by a small, intimate studio setting. Acoustical guitars and pianos replace electric instruments. With the cacophony of laser lights and overpowering high-tech sound effects unplugged, the music and its message are all that remain. The music is reduced to its essence.

The results of this new cultural movement have been varied. Some concerts are powerful, others are pathetic. In either case, the unplugged music reveals its true essence. Similarly, *The Gospel Unplugged* strips away the distractions of complex theological banter and religious debate to reveal the essence of the Gospel—the plain and simple *Good News*.

Perhaps you are troubled by all of the bad news in the world today and are searching for answers. Maybe you have never really heard about God's amazing good news and your curiosity has been peaked. Could this be the good news you have been looking for? If so, then this book is for you.

Or perhaps you have already heard the good news about Christ and trusted Him to be your Savior. If so, this book will benefit you as well. We all need to be reminded of the basics of the game sometimes. It will help us share the good news with others more accurately and confidently.

In the pages that follow we will learn many things about God and His plan to overcome all of the bad news with good news. First we will see that as bad as things are, there is *even worse news*. The really bad news is not about what is happening on earth. The really bad news is that the source of all of the evil we see happening around us is a problem called *sin*. Sin has separated us from God and there is nothing we can do on our own to solve the problem. We all face a terrible predicament that has eternal consequences if left unremedied.

But we will also learn some amazing good news in this book. We will see that God has provided a solution to our sin problem that is absolutely free if we will simply receive it. It is called the Gospel. In the pages that follow, we will examine the Gospel and discover that it really is good news—*very good news*—plain and simple.

1

READ THE FINE PRINT

"Trust everybody, but cut the cards!"
(Mark Twain)

"There is no such thing as a free lunch." This well known axiom reflects a deep-seated skepticism shared by most people today. It's a skepticism that causes us to doubt the sincerity and legitimacy of every *good deal* no matter how attractive or compelling it may appear to be at first glance. Even the most naïve among us knows to read the fine print before signing on the proverbial dotted line.

Things are seldom as advertised. Perhaps nothing illustrates this better than a recent ad campaign by a leading pizza chain. Here is how the "deal" is promoted in the company's TV commercials:

- $10 for *any* pizza!
- *Any* size
- *Any* number of toppings
- *Any* crust

Sounds like a great deal, right? Any size … any number of toppings … any crust. How could there possibly be any wiggle room in that?

That's what I thought too. But if you call your neighborhood franchise you'll discover that despite the all-inclusive language in the TV commercial, there are nevertheless *exceptions*. "There is an additional charge," you will be told, "for stuffed crust." You can argue with the person on the other end of the phone as I did, but to no avail.

"That's not what the commercial says!" you will protest.

"Read the fine print," you will be told.

Sure enough, the next time you watch the TV ad from the pizza company, you will see a very small notation briefly appearing at the bottom of the screen: "Stuffed crust $1 additional charge." Amazing!

You missed it the first time because your attention was captured by the large print on the screen and the voice-over announcement emphasizing the "teaser rate." How can they get away with saying, "*Any* pizza... *any* size... *any* number of toppings... *any* crust" when in reality at least one kind of crust is *excluded*? The answer lies in our current culture's willingness to embrace abstraction and imprecision.

What Can You Really Count On?

> Our world today is far more comfortable with vagueness and ambiguity than at any other time in human history.

Our world today is far more comfortable with vagueness and ambiguity than at any other time in human history. In fact, there has been a profound abandonment of certainty in the hearts and minds of most people. Any principle or belief that is asserted with dogmatism and certainty is instinctively questioned and usually dismissed out of hand. Anything *that* certain must not be true!

Thus when a pizza chain makes a promise using absolute language, and the customer later realizes he has been the victim of a bait and switch, he simply shrugs his shoulders and says, "Well... okay... if you say so." We have become conditioned to accept contradictions and violations of language without holding people accountable to the inherent meaning of the original promise. Scholars call this tendency toward more ambiguity and less certainty *pluralism*. In essence, pluralism is the view that two or more contradictory statements can be true at the same time.

Not only has pluralism given rise to the abandonment of certainty in general, but it has had a serious impact on language in particular. In days gone by, when someone wanted to affirm the certainty of a statement, he might assert, "It's the Gospel truth!" Yet today such a statement stands as a meaningless redundancy; both "Gospel" and "truth" have become ambiguous.

This absence of meaning in language is what experts call *deconstructionism*, and it represents a serious and dangerous foe for our culture. In a world where truth is relative, words likewise are relative. Just as truth is an individual construction, so too is the meaning of words. Words are made to mean whatever you need them to mean at the moment. Meaning no longer exists as an inherent end in itself. Rather, the search for meaning is like the endless pursuit of a moving target.

Perception wins the day over reality. As one writer put it, "The trouble with our age is that it is all signpost and no destination." Spin is literally everything. The make-up artist is more important than the speech writer. It is all theater and no substance. Facts are no longer relevant; what matters most is what matters to me. With language losing its meaning, truth is always an open-ended subject.

The nineteenth-century German atheist and philosopher Friedrich Nietzsche once remarked, "I fear we are not getting rid of God because we still believe in grammar." Could it be that when the lights dim on our generation, grammar may indeed have gone the way of all flesh leaving no empirical means to facilitate communication? Let's hope not. The Bible is clear that we can "know the *certainty* of the words of truth" (Prov 22:21).

Too Good to Be True

The emptiness of words in our culture has had a tragic impact on man's search for Truth. We all long for something we can count on. Yet with so many disappointments and contradictions surrounding us everyday—so many that we have come to expect them—many people have developed a profound cynicism when it comes to religion.

That's understandable.

And it explains why many people jump from one spiritual interest to another without ever finding lasting peace.

It also explains why the one true answer to man's problems often is dismissed out of hand because it seems too good to be true. It seems too simple. Too clear. Too plain. There *must* be more complexity to it.

The pursuit of peace, significance, reality, and truth … is it all a hopeless journey? I don't believe so. Isn't there some stake in the ground … some anchor to which we can remain tethered as we navigate this hazy, complex world? I think there is.

Join me as we journey through the Bible to discover the good news. No strings attached. No fine print. No hidden fees or contracts. Just good news, plain and simple.

• • •

Chapter One Discussion Questions

1.   What is *pluralism*?

2.   Why do you suppose people are so willing to accept competing worldviews as being equally valid?

3.   What is *deconstructionism*?

4.   Why is language important?

5.   How does the deconstruction of language affect our
      ability to communicate with one another?

2

CHOOSE THE RIGHT PLAYBOOK

"Some books are to be tasted, others to be swallowed,
and some few to be chewed and digested."
(Francis Bacon)

What is the greatest book you have ever read? Think back through time... through your childhood elementary school days. Think about books your mother or father may have read to you. What about books you read as a teenager? What book stands out in your mind as a favorite, and what is it about that book that left an indelible impression in your mind? What makes a book great?

It is not the amount of sales, nor its ranking on the *New York Times Bestseller List* that certifies a book as great. What makes a book great is that you still remember it long after you have put it down. A great book leaves its mark on the reader.

Without question, the greatest book ever written is the Bible. Written over a period of approximately 1500 years, beginning some fifteen centuries before Christ, by 40 or more different human authors in three different languages, the Bible contains God's blueprint for human history.

It begins with the origin of man and ends with the destiny of man. And in between it tells the wonderful news of the redemption of man. And it does it all with such amazing continuity, consistency and truly miraculous accuracy that the only possible explanation is that the Bible is a *supernatural book*. It has been said that when you read any book on the planet, *you are doing something to it.* But when you read the Bible, *it is doing something to you!*

That is because the Bible is living and active. It is the very *Word of God.* Although God used human authors to compose the pages of His Word, and although they each wrote according to their own unique styles and personalities, God's Holy Spirit carried them along so that what they wrote was in perfect accord with truth.

> "The Bible is a phenomenon which is explainable in but one way—it is the Word of God. It is not such a book as man would write if he *could*, or could write if he *would*."
> (Lewis Sperry Chafer)

The words of the Bible cut straight through all of the convoluted and confusing musings of the human heart.

The words of the Bible cut straight through all of the convoluted and confusing musings of the human heart. With surgical precision, the Bible separates fact from fiction. The Bible's words convict, draw and compel us. More than 3800 times the Bible declares "Thus says the Lord." It is the very self-revelation of God. And *every Word of God is flawless* (Prov 30:5).

We live in an age where information is rapidly and uncontrollably expanding. Pervasive WiFi connectivity, digital technology, e-mail, social networking, smart phones, Twitter, YouTube, etc., have made instant access to information commonplace. The information superhighway is changing the way knowledge is spread throughout our culture. The problem is there is no mutually agreed upon authority to police this superhighway. That is why choosing the right Playbook is so critical.

The Grand Unveiling

Picture in your mind a room filled with people from the high society crowd. They have gathered in an upscale penthouse for a very special occasion: the unveiling of a long awaited sculpture by a world famous sculptor. Off in the corner sits the masterpiece hidden by a large canvas sheet.

At the appointed time, the master of ceremonies gets everyone's attention as he taps his champagne glass with his dessert spoon. Everyone's eyes turn toward the sculpture as they wait with baited breath for the work of art to be unveiled. After a few more breathless moments, the sheet is removed and everyone can clearly see what the master-sculptor had been working on for many months.

Similarly, God revealed Himself to mankind over a period of 1500 years through the written Word. We call this the Bible. It is God's self-unveiling. God ripped away the sheet and has given us a glimpse at His creative-redemptive plan for the world. The Bible is God saying, "Here I am. Look at Me."

The Bible is God saying, "Here I am. Look at Me."

True, God also has revealed himself in other, more general ways, such as nature, providence, and human conscience. But the search for absolute truth begins and ends with the Bible. The Bible is the *only standard* for our beliefs, attitudes and practices. That means that where our beliefs or behaviors may differ from the principles contained in the Bible, *we are the ones who must change*. Truth never changes.

That is why the devil's first official act in interacting with mankind was to question God's Word. "Did God really say that?" the devil asked Eve in the Garden (Gen 3:1). Satan knows that when we stick with God's Playbook, he does not stand a chance. Every Word of God is flawless. When we ignore the Bible, or question it, or marginalize it, we do so at our own peril, for we are playing right into the devil's hands.

Everything You Need to Know for Life

The Bible is like a flawless Playbook where every play works without a hitch. The Bible has withstood the ravages of time, the revolution of change and the scrutiny of skeptics. The Playbook of God's Word reminds us that its guidelines are profitable to help us become mature and successfully navigate the waters of life. Specifically, the Bible tells us (1) what to believe; (2) what *not* to believe; (3) how to behave; and (4) how *not* to behave (See 2 Tim 3:16-17). When you boil it all down, what more is there to life?

We need to know how to behave. What behaviors are ideal and certain to lead to blessings in life? We need to know how *not* to behave. What behaviors are risky and likely to lead to unpleasant experiences and negative consequences? We need to know what to believe and what *not* to believe. What is true and what is not true? How can we recognize error and deception? These are the fundamental issues of life, and all of them are contained within the Playbook—*the Bible.*

> "The purpose of God in providing the Bible is that man, to whom the Bible is addressed, may be possessed of dependable information regarding things tangible and intangible, temporal and eternal, visible and invisible, earthly and heavenly. In view of man's native limitations, *this fund of truth is of measureless value to him."*
> (Lewis Sperry Chafer)

Hundreds of years before Christ, the Psalmist spoke of the value of following the principles contained in the Bible. He said that we can cleanse our behavior and keep from sinning against God by following His Word (Psalm 119:9, 11). James, the Lord's brother, echoed those thoughts in the early days after Christ's crucifixion and resurrection. "If we are doers of the Word," he said, "we will be blessed in all that we do" (James 1:22-25).

In the next chapter, we will examine the Playbook in greater detail to learn more about the specific game plan for life. What exactly is this *good news* you've heard so much about?

. . .

Chapter Two Discussion Questions

1. What is the ultimate standard for our beliefs, attitudes and behaviors?

2. What makes the Bible such a unique book?

3.   What do we mean when we describe the Bible as God's "self-unveiling?"

4.   Can the Bible be trusted?

5. What is the result of following God's Playbook?

3

UNDERSTAND THE GAME PLAN

"You shall know the truth, and the truth shall make you free."
(Jesus Christ)

If we dig a little deeper into the Playbook, we will notice that a specific game plan emerges. While there are many important principles in the Bible to assist us with everything from marriage, to finances, to raising children, to successful business and more, the most vital information contained within this Book pertains to your personal game plan for life.

The Bible calls this game plan for life the *Gospel*. The word *gospel* comes from a Greek word that means *good news*. Although the word is used in various contexts throughout Scripture, when it comes to your personal game plan for life, the term *Gospel* refers to the good news about eternal salvation. And there is *nothing more important in all of life than the good news about eternal salvation*. The Gospel is what matters most!

What Matters Most

Allow me to paint a picture in your mind. It is a bright, sunny day. A gentle breeze is blowing. It's not too hot or cold—just an overall pleasant day. So you decide to embark on a joyride through the countryside to take in the scenery. As you are driving down a country road, you come upon a roadside sign that reads, *Caution! This sign has sharp edges on it. Do not touch the edges of this sign.* Speeding past the sign, you think to yourself, "How odd! Why would someone put a sign like that up on the road? That is really weird. It must be some kind of joke."

Moments later, still querying in your mind about the odd sign, you find the front end of your car barreling over a bridge that has been washed out by a recent rainstorm. Your car begins to sink in a muddy creek and you barely escape with your life. Walking back down the road to seek help, you once again come upon that strange sign. But this time you notice some small print at the very bottom of the sign that you had not noticed as you zoomed past at 50 MPH. You walk up to the sign and discover that the fine print reads: *By the way, the bridge is out up ahead!*

Can you imagine the indignation you would feel?! Someone took the time to manufacture a wonderful, smooth, shiny, reflective sign with good and accurate information about the sign's sharp edges. But they failed to emphasize what mattered most!

And so it is with Christianity these days. We have forgotten what matters most: The Gospel! Or at least we seem to have forgotten. Just take a quick look at the best-selling Christian books. Or listen to the radio programs of leading evangelical personalities. Or spend a few minutes watching TBN on cable. You will notice plenty of wonderful, smooth, shiny, reflective information that is in many cases good and accurate, but often what matters most is ignored, or worse yet, dead wrong.

The Gospel is foundational to Christianity. No subject is more important in the Bible. And yet in this contemporary culture where we are inclined to draw circles of inclusion rather than lines of distinction, many people seem unwilling or unable to critically evaluate the accuracy of the gospel being preached. It is easy to become enamored with Christian leaders whose teaching on certain subjects is deemed encouraging and beneficial, while winking and nodding at the same teacher's erroneous view of the Gospel.

"He is such a passionate speaker!" But is he correct when it comes to what matters most? "He is an expert on financial issues." But is he correct when it comes to what matters most? "She is a gifted communicator on family matters." But is she correct when it comes to what matters most? "This book on marriage is the best I've ever read!" But is the author correct when it comes to what matters most?

What matters most is the Gospel.

What matters most is the Gospel. It does not matter how committed someone may be to other good issues, if he is wrong on the Gospel his wisdom and insight are built upon a faulty foundation.

The Bible says that those who are preaching a false gospel are *anathema* (Gal 1:8-9). Literally, that word means "worthy of severe judgment "or "deserving of destruction." The word does not, in and of itself, imply that the one preaching a false gospel is hell-bound himself—though he could be if he has never believed the pure Gospel. The fact is even Christians can come under strict judgment (1 Cor. 16:22). And the Bible makes it clear that God is severely displeased by those who propagate a false Gospel. What form the severe judgment will take is entirely up to God.

Why then would we ever want to promote or follow those whom God describes as being anathematized? It is really bizarre when you stop and think about it:

"Can you recommend a good book on finances?"

"Sure! Try this book by so-and-so. God says the author is worthy of severe judgment, but hey, he has a lot of great insight on how to manage your money!"

What matters most is the Gospel. If we forget that simple fact, we are in danger of plummeting right off the bridge into muddy creek waters. And while we are drowning in sin, it really won't matter that we have a great marriage, or that our finances are in order, or that we are living our best life now. Knowing the game plan for life involves being able to prioritize what matters most. And what matters most is *the Gospel*!

God's Good News

As we said at the beginning of this chapter, the *Gospel* is the good news of man's eternal salvation. This good news touches on three key facts. In the first place it addresses the bad news that man is a sinner in need of a Savior. We will call this the *predicament*.

Secondly, it presents the good news that God has provided this Savior through His Son, who died and rose again. We will call this the *provision*.

Finally, the good news about man's eternal salvation explains precisely how we can appropriate God's provision through His Son. What specifically must we do to gain the forgiveness of sins and eternal life? More than 200 times the Bible is clear that the only means of obtaining eternal life is faith alone in Christ alone. We will call this the *profession*.

Thus the Gospel encompasses man's *predicament*, God's *provision* and individual *profession*. Let's take a closer look at these three aspects of the Gospel.

> **"Preaching the Gospel is telling men something about Christ and His finished work for them, which they are to believe. This is the simplest test to be applied to all soul-saving appeals. The Gospel has not been preached until a personal message concerning a crucified and living Saviour has been presented, and in a form which calls for the response of a personal faith."**
> **(Lewis Sperry Chafer)**

The Predicament

It is surprising how little attention is paid to the reality of sin in our contemporary culture. Sin has been redefined.

It is surprising how little attention is paid to the reality of sin in our contemporary culture.

It is no longer couched in terms of moral absolutes. We are more comfortable using words like *weakness* or *limitation* or *flaw*. After all, *sin* is such an ugly word. It sounds so judgmental and critical. In a world with no absolutes, who's to say what is sin and what is not?

Yet in spite of our culture's disdain for anything absolute, sin is a serious reality that must be addressed. The Gospel message in the New Testament occurs in the context of man's sinfulness. It begins with the premise: *man is a sinner in need of a Savior.* One of the most famous biblical authors, the Apostle Paul, spends three chapters in his famous doctrinal treatise to the Romans establishing the fact that mankind is in trouble. We have all "sinned and fallen short of the glory of God" (Rom 3:23).

Not only has the term *sin* been redefined, but the consequences of sin have been marginalized. When the bad news is downplayed or ignored altogether, it makes the good news less relevant. Indeed, what makes the Gospel message *good news* is that it solves man's predicament. Man's sinfulness, if not remedied, results in eternity in a literal place of torment called hell. "For the wages of sin is death ..." (Rom 6:23a).

> "It is sin that has drawn out redemption from the heart of God, and redemption is the only cure for sin. These two realities, in turn, become measurements of each other. *Where sin is minimized, redemption is automatically impoverished since its necessity is by so much decreased.* The worthy approach to the doctrine of sin is to discover all that is revealed about the sinfulness of sin and then to recognize that God's provided Savior is equal to every demand which sin imposes."
> **(Lewis Sperry Chafer)**

> Only the most self-deceived individual would claim that he or she is perfect.

Ignorance about sin does not excuse one from the predicament. According to the Bible, all men are without excuse when it comes to salvation because of God's general revelation (Rom 1:18–32; Ps 19:1; Acts 14:17). In other words, deep down inside, we all know that we are sinners. Only the most self-deceived individual would claim that he or she is perfect.

Before you can receive eternal salvation by faith alone in Christ alone, you must first acknowledge the specific nature of your predicament—namely, that your personal sinfulness has consigned you to hell. It's a heavy thought, I know. That is why the Gospel is such great news!

The Provision

The Gospel announces the solution to humanity's predicament. Jesus Christ, the sinless Son of God, paid the penalty for mankind by dying on the cross. He rose again the third day and freely offers deliverance from hell and the gift of eternal life to all. "…the gift of God is eternal life through Jesus Christ our Lord" (Rom 6:23b).

> "Scripture discloses the fact that the power and resources of God are more taxed by all that enters into the salvation of the soul than His power and resources were taxed in the creation of the material universe. In salvation God has wrought to the extreme limit of His might. He spared not His own Son, but delivered Him up for us all. *He could do no more.*"
>
> **(Lewis Sperry Chafer)**

Jesus is our substitute. That means it should have been you and me on that cross, but He took our place. Bible scholars refer to this concept as the *substitutionary atonement* of Christ. It is hard to wrap our minds around this concept because we live in such an ego-centric culture. The Bible anticipated that it would be hard for people to believe in the Gospel. "For scarcely for a righteous man will one die; yet perhaps for a good man someone would even dare to die. But God demonstrates His own love toward us, in that while we were still sinners, Christ died for us" (Romans 5:7–8).

That is the very essence of grace. *God's Riches at Christ's Expense.* What does the term *grace* mean to you? Have you ever thought about it? To many people, grace is something you say before a meal; or the way you describe a beautiful ballet dancer; or extra time to make your credit card payment. But the biblical word grace refers to a *free gift* offered by God to mankind. We are "justified freely by His grace through the redemption that is in Christ Jesus" (Romans 3:24).

The word *justified* means to be declared righteous. When we trust in Christ, our predicament is solved. We are declared righteous by God, and it is just as if we had never sinned. We are clothed in Christ's righteousness. "Having been justified by faith, we have peace with God through our Lord Jesus Christ" (Romans 5:1).

Make no mistake … there was a high cost for this gift. It cost God His one and only Son. It cost God's Son his very life. But it does not cost us *anything*. That is because Jesus paid our debt. Eternal salvation is a *free gift*. That is so counter-intuitive to what we have been taught that it bears repeating. *Eternal salvation is a free gift.* That's what grace means (Rom 5:12-21).

> *"The resources of language have been exhausted in the attempt to indicate the infinite grace of God in terms of human speech.* **Probably these resources of language have been more exhausted at this point than concerning any other theme of the Word of God. How could it be otherwise? God through grace purposes the realization of the greatest undertaking and accomplishment in all the universe."**
> **(Lewis Sperry Chafer)**

Although the penalty for sin is horrifying, the remedy is sufficient.

Although the penalty for sin is horrifying, the remedy is sufficient. All hope is not lost. The provision has been made. As we will see in the following pages, all that remains is for the sinner to accept it. No strings attached. That really is *good news*—plain and simple.

The Profession

But how exactly do we accept this provision? Is it automatic? Is it something we earn? Earlier we saw how the Bible refers to God's provision in sending His Son to die for us as a "gift." This should give us a clue as to how we accept His provision.

Like any gift, we must accept it. The Bible says that only those who receive the gift of salvation provided by God's Son will actually be rescued from hell and have eternal life. And the way we receive the gift of eternal life is by *faith* (John 1:12).

Jesus said, "Whoever *believes* in Me has everlasting life" (John 6:47). The instrumentality of faith in securing eternal salvation is undeniable in Scripture. More than 200 times the Bible conditions eternal life upon faith alone. Nothing else. As the great hymn writer put it, "Nothing in my hand I bring.

Simply to the cross I cling." Jesus really did pay it all. He paid a debt He did not owe. And we owed a debt we could never pay.

Our only hope is to trust in Jesus. No amount of good works, good intentions or self-help programs can overcome our sin problem. Only a sinless Savior can do that. And He did so when He took my sin and your sin upon Himself at Calvary.

Our only hope is to trust in Jesus.

When Jesus died and rose again for our sins, He defeated death, hell and the grave and thus has the right to offer to all who will accept it the free gift of eternal life.

Life Is Not a Game of Go Fish

Sometime ago, I was playing a game of *Go Fish* with my son, Landry, who was eight years old at the time. It is quite entertaining to watch a child's mind at work. This particular game of *Go Fish* was especially fun because the cards were not the usual numbered playing cards. Instead, they contained a variety of photos—a bicycle, a raincoat, flowers, a lobster, etc. I could see Landry's wheels turning as he drew cards and narrowed down the possibilities.

"Do you have any c-l-o-w-n-s?" Landry asked, emphasizing the key word by saying it slowly.

"Go fish," I replied. Then I asked, "Do you have any skateboards?"

"Ugh! How did you know?" he moaned. And back and forth we went until one of us (usually him) emptied his hand of all his cards. Such fun—especially the look on a child's face when he wins!

It occurs to me that many people go through life as if it were a game of *Go Fish*. They evaluate their lives, try to figure out what is missing, and then fill that void with what appears to correspond to their need at the moment. Lonely? Go fish. (Hand me another drink.) Need self-esteem? Go fish. (Tear others down to hide my own insecurity.) Need a new TV or nicer car? Go fish. (Spend money I don't have.) Looking for meaning or purpose in life? Go fish. (Read another book by Dr. Phil.)

But life is not a game of *Go Fish*. No matter how long you play; no matter how many times you draw, you will never find true contentment drawing from the world's stack of cards. The stack is never ending. There will always be more cards to draw.

That is because, as the Bible reminds us, to the hungry soul every bitter thing seems sweet (Prov 27:7). But to those who have found true peace with God, even the sweetest honey will have no appeal.

> No amount of good works, self-effort, or morally upstanding behavior can overcome your predicament.

No amount of good works, self-effort, or morally upstanding behavior can overcome your predicament. The only remedy for sin is faith alone in Christ alone. The Bible makes it clear that any good works we may conjure up in our own efforts are like filthy rags when compared to the perfect holiness of God (Isa 64:6).

> "Grace is neither treating a person as he deserves, nor treating a person better than he deserves, but treating a person *without the slightest reference to what he deserves*."
> (Lewis Sperry Chafer)

Is it your turn to draw? Let me encourage you to set the cards aside and turn to the Gospel as the only real solution to life's problems. No matter what you are facing, the Bible has the answers. Within its pages we find the game plan—everything we need for life and godliness. Most importantly, the Bible introduces us to Jesus Christ, the Son of God, who died for our sins and rose again. He is the Way, the Truth and the Life. In Him is life, and that life is the Light of men. In Him we can have abundant life.

Have you trusted in Jesus Christ to forgive your sin and give you the free gift of eternal life? If not, the time to do so is now...before the game ends and you lose. If you already have a relationship with Christ by faith, let me encourage you to resist the temptation to join that old *Go Fish* game. Instead of reaching for that futile deck of cards, pick up the Bible instead. It will satisfy your every need.

• • •

Chapter Three Discussion Questions

1.   What is the most important issue in life?

2.   What serious predicament does every human being face?

3. What is God's solution to our predicament?

4. Is there anything we can do to earn eternal life?

5.   According to the Bible, what is God's *grace*?

4
KNOW THE FACTS

"Facts do not cease to exist because they are ignored."
(Aldous Huxley)

Thus far we have established that there is only one Playbook that counts: The Bible. And we have determined that the Bible's game plan involves a terrible predicament: sin and its eternal consequences. It also involves a wonderful provision: Jesus Christ and His sacrificial death on the cross. Finally, we learned about the profession of faith: The only means of accepting this free gift is faith alone in Christ alone.

In this chapter we will examine some very important details about God's Game Plan. We will discover precisely what you have to believe about Jesus in order to receive eternal life. These facts are crucial. We ignore them at our own peril. So let me encourage you to read carefully. This may be the most important chapter you will ever read.

Turn Down the Volume So You Can Hear

Every year, my wife and I enjoy taking our six children to the Houston Livestock Show and Rodeo. It is always an eventful and fun outing. By nearly unanimous vote, our family's favorite event is bull riding. Typically only one or two cowboys manage to hang on for the entire eight seconds. What fun it is to see the look in the kids' eyes and the expressions on their faces as they watch the events unfold in the arena. For me, it is even more fun listening to their comments.

If you know anything about being in a large sports arena with 50,000 screaming fans, you know how hard it can be to carry on a conversation—even with a person sitting right next to you. And if you know anything about our son Morgan, you know of his decidedly uninhibited outlook on life and the correspondingly transparent comments such an outlook engenders. During one of our annual visits to the rodeo, Morgan leaned over to me and shouted above the deafening din of the crowd, "Dad! All this noise is great. I can burp really loud and nobody can hear me!"

It's true. Sometimes the volume can be *too loud* to hear. It is counterintuitive, really. We normally think of turning the volume *up* when we can't hear it. But if it is too loud, it distorts the message and may very well drown out other important information. Not that a burp is particularly important, but you get the idea.

> Often our focus can be so distracted by the hustle and bustle of life, by the deafening din of everyday activities, that we miss the most important message.

And so it is with our spiritual lives as well. Often our focus can be so distracted by the hustle and bustle of life, by the deafening din of everyday activities, that we miss the most important message. That was the case with Israel many centuries before Christ. The leaders of Israel were engaged in loud and intense conversations among themselves and with other nations in an effort to defend themselves against enemy attacks. But the Lord reminded them through the Psalmist that if they would only stop striving, God would be their refuge and strength.

"Be still!" God said, "And know that I am God. I will take care of you. I will be your refuge. I will defend you and exalt My Name above all the earth" (Psalm 46:10). The verb "be still" is a Hebrew word that literally means "stop fighting so hard." Do you realize that many people fight hard for the wrong cause? It is all too easy to get distracted by the cacophonous sounds of life as they drown out the truth.

> **"...there is need of great clearness and skill in explaining the exact terms of the Gospel to the one upon whom the Spirit is moving in conviction and illumination."**
> **(Lewis Sperry Chafer)**

When it comes to the Gospel, there is only one message that results in eternal salvation when we believe it. The Bible tells us that the Gospel is "the power of God to salvation" to everyone who *believes it*. If we believe the wrong message, the power to save is not present. So what is that message, precisely? Read on.

The Irreducible Minimum

The term *irreducible minimum* is how one Christian writer refers to the precise content of saving faith. I think this is a great way to put it. In other words, there are many things about Christ that are revealed in the Bible, but not all of these result in eternal salvation to those who believe them. For instance, it is true that Jesus fed the 5,000, but believing this historical fact does not impart eternal salvation. Similarly, it is true that Jesus was born in Bethlehem, but again, believing this historical fact does not result in eternal salvation.

By *irreducible minimum*, we are referring to the precise content of saving faith. It is that content without which your faith will *not* result in eternal salvation. We might call it the *kernel of salvific truth*. What is about Christ that, when believed, results in eternal salvation (Rom 1:16).

In this current climate of ambiguity, many people—even some Christian leaders—are uncomfortable couching the saving message of the Gospel in such precise terms. The term *irreducible minimum* is especially off-putting to them because of its inherent narrow nuance. Yet, it is difficult to see why this phrase would be a concern.

The issue at hand is: Is it possible for a person to know what he has to believe in order to receive eternal life? The answer to this question, of course, has to be *yes*! This is because if it is not possible to know what we have to believe to be saved, then no one could ever be saved. Since it is in fact possible to know what you have to believe in order to receive eternal life, then the natural and necessary follow–up to that question is: "What is it?" What is the precise content of saving faith?

At a time when many people have grown quite comfortable with ambiguity and uncertainty, it is crucial that we accurately quantify the biblical content of saving faith. But first, we must define what we mean by *saving faith*.

> At a time when many people have grown quite comfortable with ambiguity and uncertainty, it is crucial that we accurately quantify the biblical content of saving faith.

Saving Faith

Quite simply, saving faith refers to *faith that results in eternal salvation*. We can and do believe many things. For example, I believe the Dallas Cowboys are the best NFL football team. That's faith … but it is not *saving faith*. A child might believe in Santa Claus. That is faith … but it is not *saving faith*. I believe that the Bill of Rights provide (or at least used to provide) the foundational elements of freedom in our country. That is faith … but it is not *saving faith*.

Saving faith occurs the moment *faith* meets the *correct object*. Since neither the Dallas Cowboys, nor Santa Claus nor one's view on the Bill of Rights have anything to do with the irreducible minimum of the Gospel, faith in those things cannot result in eternal salvation. What results in eternal salvation is faith in the *correct object*—the kernel of salvific truth. It is the *Gospel* that is the power of God to salvation when you believe it. And the *Gospel* has clearly specific content.

While some have suggested that it is the *kind* of faith that saves rather than its precise *object*, such a notion is not found anywhere in the Bible. Faith is faith. You either believe something or you do not. It is not the *quality* of our faith that saves us. Indeed, the Bible makes it clear that even very small faith—faith the size of a mustard seed—can result in eternal salvation, so long as it is in the right object.

> "...salvation is through Christ alone...
> it is secured, on the human side, by faith alone
> uncomplicated by any works of merit."
> **(Lewis Sperry Chafer)**

No, it is not the kind or quality of faith that matters. What brings eternal salvation is *faith in the correct object*. When faith meets the right object the result is saving faith. But this brings up another question. What does it mean to have faith? What is *faith*, in and of itself?

Faith

The concept of faith is actually quite simple. To believe something is to be certain that it is true. Faith is the very evidence of what we cannot see. We might call this *generic faith*,

> **Where there is doubt, there is no faith. And where there is faith, there is no doubt.**

as opposed to *saving faith*. Generic faith is faith in *anything*. Saving faith is faith in the *Gospel*, which brings eternal life. If you doubt the truthfulness of a promise or proposition, then you have not believed it. Doubt and faith—by definition—cannot coexist. Where there is doubt, there is no faith. And where there is faith, there is no doubt.

Generic faith is the *assurance or confidence in some stated or implied truth*. This truth may be in the form of a simple *proposition*—I believe the earth is round. Or it may be in the form of a *person* with one or more propositions inseparably wrapped up in that person—I believe George Washington was the first American president. In either case, when you believe something, by definition you are certain of its truthfulness or reliability at that moment.

Of course, it is possible for you to believe something and later change your mind; and it is also possible for you to believe something and be wrong about your belief. A child's belief in Santa Claus is no less real than a parent's belief that Santa Claus is a myth. Both involve faith. One is correct, the other is not. But in any event, to believe something or someone (i.e., have faith in it, trust it) is to put your unwavering confidence in its trustworthiness.

The Essence of Saving Faith

Having defined what we mean by *saving faith* and how it is distinguished from *generic faith*, we now come to the crux of the matter. What precisely must someone believe in order for that faith to be deemed *saving faith*? That is, what is the essence of saving faith?

Even someone who is only remotely familiar with Christianity would agree that faith in Jesus is necessary for eternal salvation. But what does this mean exactly? Is it enough merely to believe that Jesus exists? The phrase "believe in Jesus" is ambiguous without further qualifying information. In fact, it is impossible to have faith in a person without also understanding and believing certain propositions associated with that person.

For instance, the isolated statement, "I believe in Jim," absent of any corresponding propositional assertions, is meaningless. Such an ambiguous statement immediately begs such questions as, "*What* do you believe about Jim?" Or, "*What* do you believe Jim will *do?*" Or, "*Who* is Jim anyway?"

Similarly, it is not enough to say merely, "believe in Jesus" if the name Jesus has no context or meaning to the audience. Therefore, it is necessary to identify certain propositional truths about Christ that are essential to the gospel. By propositional, we simply mean "clear statements regarding a matter;" in other words, clear truthful statements made about something. In the case of the Gospel, these are clear statements regarding the matters of Jesus Christ and His work of salvation.

> Similarly, it is not enough to say merely, "believe in Jesus" if the name Jesus has no context or meaning to the audience.

Does this over-intellectualize and complicate saving faith as some people claim? Let's reason this together. Propositional truths pinpoint and identify. Since saving faith involves a personal trust in the correct object, it is paramount to one's salvation and life to correctly identify the object of trust. How does one pinpoint the correct object in which to place one's trust? The only way to do this is by way of propositional truths. Since that's the case, we must be cautious of being anti-intellectualists so that we can clearly understand and discern biblical truth – that we may clearly know the requirements for a pure gospel and the conditions for eternal salvation.

Let's go back to the game plan and take a closer look at the essence of saving faith. If you want to overcome the predicament of sin....if you want to avoid sin's eternal consequences...if you want to receive eternal life....*what precisely must you believe about Jesus Christ?*

Jesus is the Son of God

"Jesus, Jesus, Jesus...there's just something about that name." This favorite old hymn calls to mind the uniqueness of Jesus Christ. There is no one like Him. He is the eternal Son of God. And the Gospel message is all about *Jesus*. Any Gospel message that omits explicit reference to Jesus Christ is not good news at all. It is bad news and false information.

I'm not a big fan of bumper sticker theology, but sometimes bumper stickers get it right. And the one that comes to mind on this point is: *Know Jesus. Know Peace. No Jesus. No peace.* That is it in a nutshell.

The centrality of Jesus Christ as the object of saving faith is indisputable.

The centrality of Jesus Christ as the object of saving faith is indisputable. "For God so loved the world that He gave *His only begotten Son*, that whoever believes *in Him* should not perish but have everlasting life" (John 3:16). Jesus Himself affirmed this truth many times, "Most assuredly, I say to you, he who believes *in Me* has everlasting life" (John 6:47; see also John 6:35; 7:38; 11:25-26; 12:46; and many others).

The famous Apostle Paul inseparably links our eternal salvation with the person and work of Jesus Christ in Romans 5:8, "But God demonstrates His own love toward us, in that while we were still sinners, *Christ* died for us." And again in his response to the Philippian jailor, "Believe on the *Lord Jesus Christ,* and you will be saved, you and your household" (Acts 16:31).

The Apostle John likewise tells his readers, "And truly *Jesus* did many other signs in the presence of His disciples, which are not written in this book; but these are written that you may believe that *Jesus* is the Christ, the Son of God, and that believing you may have life in *His name*" (John 20:30–31).

The Prophet Isaiah, long before Jesus came to earth in the form of a man, referred to Jesus as the "Mighty God" and "Everlasting Father" (Isa 9:6-7). There can be no doubt that the Jesus who saves is the eternal Son of God.

To acknowledge that Jesus is the Son of God is to recognize that He is unlike any other man. He is a man; that is true. But He is not just *any* man. He is God in human flesh. Jesus "became flesh and dwelt among us, and we beheld His glory, the glory as of the only begotten of the Father, full of grace and truth" (John 1:14).

When you put your trust in Jesus Christ to give you the gift of eternal life, you must recognize that He, and He alone, has the power to forgive sin and grant life. There may be many people with the name "Jesus" in the world, but only One is the Son of God. Only One is God in the flesh. Only One. *The* Jesus. *Jesus Christ, the Son of God.* He is the One who will save you from your sins if you will simply believe in Him.

Jesus Died and Rose Again

It is not enough, though, to simply believe in Jesus as the Son of God. The Gospel message also includes the work of Christ. Remember what we said earlier. Faith in a person necessarily involves understanding key identifying propositions about that person. In the case of saving faith in Jesus Christ, we must not only recognize that He is the One and only Son of God, but also that as God He paid our penalty when He died in our place on the cross.

As strange as it may sound, there are some people who suggest you can believe in Jesus to give you eternal life without even knowing who He is or what He did for you on the cross. This idea is not only patently unbiblical, it is also illogical. Why would anyone believe in someone they know absolutely nothing about to give them eternal life? This erroneous view has been termed the *crossless gospel* because it insists that knowledge of Christ's work on the cross is optional when it comes to the essence of saving faith.

Perhaps a better label for this strange view would be the *promise-only gospel* because it makes faith in the promise of Jesus all that is necessary for salvation. But a promise is only as good as the one making it! And when it comes to the content of saving faith, the One promising eternal life is the Son of God who died and rose again for our sins. Sadly, proponents of the *crossless* view have stripped the Gospel message of critical content for salvation. Yet, the Bible is clear that saving faith includes faith in the Person *and work* of Christ.

A promise is only as good as the one making it!

> "There is but one Savior and only One who in every respect is qualified to save."
> **(Lewis Sperry Chafer)**

To believe in Jesus as the Son of God who died and rose again is to accept Him as uniquely qualified to impart eternal life (John 11:26–27). It is to understand on some level His deity, which distinguishes Him from every other person in the history of mankind. John begins his Gospel account strongly affirming the deity of Christ. "In the beginning was the Word, and the Word was with God, and *the Word was God*" (John 1:1, emphasis added). He then goes on to explain that accepting this premise is necessary if someone desires to become a child of God; that is, to obtain eternal salvation.

"He came to His own, and His own did not receive Him. But as many as *received Him*, to them He gave the right to become children of God, to those who *believe in His name*" (John 1:11–12). John equates "receiving Him" with "believing in His name." To "believe in His name" is to accept that Jesus is who

John said He is—the eternal Son of God "[who] became flesh and dwelt among us" (John 1:14).

Faith in Jesus necessarily includes the belief that He is qualified and capable of giving the very gift He promises. Saving faith connects Christ's self-identification as the Son of God with His divine ability and authority to save. To be sure, saving faith does not require some complex affirmation of a fully developed doctrine of the deity of Christ. But however rudimentary your understanding may be on the subject of His deity, you must believe that Jesus *is uniquely God's Son* and that He accomplished something that *only God could accomplish.*

Jesus' death and resurrection, more than anything else, set Him apart as unique among men. Theologically, His death and resurrection attest to His deity. In fulfillment of Old Testament prophecy, the Son of God died and rose again to pay man's penalty for sin (Psalm 16:9–11; 68:18; 110:1; Isaiah 53:4–10). The New Testament further suggests that His death and resurrection are related to His deity (Matt 12:39–40; Mark 8:31; Luke 11:29–30; 24:26; John 2:19–21; Acts 2:23–24, 29–32; 1 Corinthians 15:3–4).

The object of saving faith, then, must include the essential truth that Jesus Christ is the Son of God who died and rose again. This does not mean that one must grasp all of the theological implications and intricacies of Christ's deity; nor does it mean that one must explicitly articulate the phrase *deity of Christ* as part of his profession of faith. Rather, believing in Jesus as the Son of God means understanding that Jesus is who He said He is: the divine Son of God who alone can forgive sin and grant eternal life because He died and rose again for our sins (John 11:25–27).

Jesus Paid Our Sin Debt

Identifying Jesus as the object of saving faith necessarily involves understanding not only that He is the Son of God who died and rose again, but also the *significance of His death and resurrection*. It involves recognizing that His death and resurrection serve as the basis for His substitutionary atonement for sin.

What do we mean by *substitutionary atonement*? This theological phrase simply refers to the payment of a debt on behalf of someone else. Multiple sources affirm that this is precisely what Jesus did for us. He paid our debt. We owed a debt we could never pay. Jesus paid a debt He did not owe.

At the outset of Jesus' earthly ministry, John the Baptist declared that Jesus is "the Lamb of God who takes away the sin of the world" (John 1:29). In John 4:24, a group of Samaritans affirm that Jesus "is indeed the Christ, the Savior of the World."

Jesus Himself said, "I am the good shepherd. The good shepherd gives His life for the sheep. Therefore My Father loves Me, because I lay down My life that I may take it again" (John 10:11, 17). He also said, "[I]f you do not believe that I am He, you will die in your sins" (John 8:24).

Saving faith includes the specific content that Jesus' death and resurrection involve personal payment for sin. The general belief that Jesus died and rose again is not, in and of itself, enough to save. Even Satan himself believes Jesus rose again. He witnessed it firsthand! Rather, you must believe that Jesus died and rose again for *you personally*. You must come to the point where you acknowledge your sinfulness (the predicament) and recognize that because of *your* sin *you* should have died on the cross. You must recognize that Jesus took *your* place—He became *your* substitute—on the cross.

The Apostle Peter clearly identified this content when he challenged Cornelius' household, "To [Jesus] all the prophets witness that, through His name, whoever believes in Him will receive forgiveness of sins" (Acts 10:43). Likewise the Apostle Paul in one of his sermons proclaimed, "Therefore let it be known to you, brethren, that through this Man is preached to you *the forgiveness of sins*" (Acts 13:38).

Romans 3:10 establishes the universal fact that all have sinned. "As it is written: 'There is none righteous, no, not one.'"

So too does Romans 3:23, "For all have sinned and fall short of the glory of God."

The New Testament frequently affirms that Jesus came into the world to rescue it from the penalty of sin. For instance, the angel's announcement to Joseph regarding Jesus' birth includes the proclamation, "You shall call His name Jesus, for *He will save His people from their sins*" (Matthew 1:21). Similarly, the angelic announcement of Jesus' birth to the shepherds refers to Jesus as the *Savior,* a reference to His atoning work on the cross (Luke 2:11; cf. Isaiah 53:4–6).

Paul makes Christ's atoning work central to His incarnation, "This is a faithful saying and worthy of all acceptance, that *Christ Jesus came into the world to save sinners*" (1 Tim 1:15). And John describes Jesus as "the propitiation for our sins, and not for ours only but also for the whole world" (1 John 2:2). The word *propitiation* refers to the fact that Christ satisfied God's anger against sin when He paid sin's penalty on our behalf.

But saving faith involves recognizing not only that Jesus is the answer to the world's sin problem in general, but to *your personal sin problem* as well. There is a personal, substitutionary component to saving faith. It is not enough simply to acknowledge that Jesus died for the sins of the whole world. What about *you personally*? Have you acknowledged your own sin and received His payment on your behalf?

Before being rescued you must first recognize you are in danger. And before you can be saved you must first acknowledge you are a sinner. Absent a proper understanding of sin and its consequence, no one can express saving faith because there is no impetus to do so. It would be like expecting a person who has cancer to take chemotherapy even though he is completely unaware he has cancer!

Jesus Rescues Us from Hell and Gives Us Eternal Life

In our contemporary culture, where sin is often marginalized or watered down, it is easy to miss just how important Christ's

---

Sin's consequences are eternal.

---

substitutionary atonement is. This is no minor problem we face. Sin's consequences are eternal. Life apart from Christ is not merely less exciting or less fulfilling or otherwise downgraded in some earthly, experiential way. Life apart from Christ means an eternity in a *literal place of torment called hell.*

Jesus once addressed a crowd and warned them about the futility of focusing only on this present earthly life. He said bluntly, "And I say to you, My friends, do not be afraid of those who kill the body, and after that have no more that they can do. But I will show you whom you should fear: Fear Him who, after He has killed, has power to cast into hell; yes, I say to you, fear Him!" (Luke 12:4–5). Elsewhere, He reminds us that those who fail to receive the free gift of eternal life will hear these dreadful words one day: "Depart from Me, you cursed, into the everlasting fire prepared for the devil and his angels" (Matt 25:41).

Jesus' contrast between an unbelieving rich man and a believing beggar named Lazarus further illustrates that the eternal consequence of sin is confinement in a place of torment for those who do not believe the gospel (Luke 16:19–31). This place of torment for the unsaved is separated from the eternal dwelling place of Christians by a "great gulf" (Luke 16:26). Hell is described in Scripture as a "lake of fire" (Rev 20:15) that involves being "tormented day and night forever and ever" (Rev 20:10).

What we are saying is that the *core essence* of salvation is the fact that we are saved *from hell* and saved *into heaven.* Jesus did not die to rescue us from a boring life. Nor did He endure the cross so that we might have *a better life now.* It is true that our life is impacted immediately the moment we trust Christ. Eternal life begins on earth and continues for eternity. Eternal life for those who have trusted Christ is a present possession, not just a future hope. All of this is true. But the point of Christ's substitutionary death was to *deliver us from the eternal consequences of sin*; namely, hell! That's the real problem.

There are plenty of ways that we can find temporary relief from the troubles and trials of life. Our culture is full of self-help programs, electronic gadgets, prescription drugs, entertainment and other avenues of escapism. But there is only one way to escape hell: faith alone in Christ alone for eternal salvation.

There is only one way to escape hell: faith alone in Christ alone for eternal salvation.

Life is about more than the here and now. And if Jesus tarries His return, everyone will find this out one day. Life's ultimate statistic is the same for everyone: *one out of one will die.* Therefore the reality of our eternal destiny is no small matter.

The Bible repeatedly characterizes eternal salvation in terms that transcend this present life. Salvation passages in the Bible are rife with terms like "eternal life," "everlasting life," "never perish," "never die," etc. Consider the following passages where references to the eternal nature of salvation have been italicized for emphasis:

> "Now behold, one came and said to Him, "Good Teacher, what good thing shall I do that I may have *eternal life*?" (Matthew 19:16).

> "And these will go away into *everlasting* punishment, but the righteous into *eternal life*" (Matthew 25:46).

> "That whoever believes in Him should not perish but have *eternal life*. For God so loved the world that He gave His only begotten Son, that whoever believes in Him should not perish but have *everlasting life*" (John 3:15–16).

> "He who believes in the Son has *everlasting life*; and he who does not believe the Son shall not see life, but the wrath of God abides on him" (John 3:36).

"Most assuredly, I say to you, he who hears My word and believes in Him who sent Me has *everlasting life*, and shall not come into judgment, but has passed from death into life" (John 5:24).

"And Jesus said to them, "I am the bread of life. He who comes to Me shall *never hunger*, and he who believes in Me shall *never thirst*" (John 6:35).

"And this is the will of Him who sent Me, that everyone who sees the Son and believes in Him may have *everlasting life*; and I will raise him up at the last day" (John 6:40).

"Most assuredly, I say to you, he who believes in Me *has everlasting life*" (John 6:47).

"Whoever eats My flesh and drinks My blood has *eternal life*, and I will raise him up at the last day" (John 6:54).

"This is the bread which came down from heaven—not as your fathers ate the manna, and are dead. He who eats this bread will *live forever*" (John 6:58).

"Most assuredly, I say to you, if anyone keeps My word he shall *never see death*" (John 8:51).

"And I give them *eternal life*, and they shall *never perish*; neither shall anyone snatch them out of My hand" (John 10:28).

"And whoever lives and believes in Me shall *never die*. Do you believe this?" (John 11:26).

"As You have given Him authority over all flesh, that He should give *eternal life* to as many as You have given Him. And this is *eternal life*, that they may know You, the only true God, and Jesus Christ whom You have sent" (John 17:2–3).

"Then Paul and Barnabas grew bold and said, "It was necessary that the word of God should be spoken to you first; but since you reject it, and judge yourselves unworthy of *everlasting life*, behold, we turn to the Gentiles" (Acts 13:46).

"Now when the Gentiles heard this, they were glad and glorified the word of the Lord. And as many as had been appointed to *eternal life* believed" (Acts 13:48).

"So that as sin reigned in death, even so grace might reign through righteousness to *eternal life* through Jesus Christ our Lord" (Romans 5:21).

"But now having been set free from sin, and having become slaves of God, you have your fruit to holiness, and the end, *everlasting life*. For the wages of sin is death, but the gift of God is *eternal life* in Christ Jesus our Lord" (Romans 6:22–23).

"However, for this reason I obtained mercy, that in me first Jesus Christ might show all longsuffering, as a pattern to those who are going to believe on Him for *everlasting life*" (1 Timothy 1:16).

"Paul, a bondservant of God and an apostle of Jesus Christ, according to the faith of God's elect and the acknowledgment of the truth which accords with godliness, in hope of *eternal life* which God, who cannot lie, promised before time began" (Titus 1:1–2).

"That having been justified by His grace we should become heirs according to the hope of *eternal life*" (Titus 3:7).

"That which was from the beginning, which we have heard, which we have seen with our eyes, which we have looked upon, and our hands have handled, concerning the Word of life— the life was manifested, and we have seen, and bear witness, and declare to you that *eternal life* which was with the Father and was manifested to us" (1 John 1:1–2).

"And this is the promise that He has promised us— *eternal life*" (1 John 2:25).

"And this is the testimony: that God has given us *eternal life*, and this life is in His Son. He who has the Son has life; he who does not have the Son of God does not have life. These things I have written to you who believe in the name of the Son of God, that you may know that you have *eternal life...*" (1 John 5:11–13).

These passages provide ample evidence to confirm that the essence of eternal salvation is the receiving of eternal life. To define eternal salvation in terms that emphasize only earthly hope, meaning, or purpose in this life to the exclusion of the eternal aspect, as many people tend to do in our current culture, is to eviscerate it, change its essential nature, and transform it into a subjective experience focused entirely on man's feelings, emotions, and present, temporal existence.

I recall the day I trusted Christ to forgive my sin and give me the free gift of eternal life. I was six years old. It was a Sunday night and I had just heard my preacher warn about the eternal consequences of sin. He said something like, "If you get hit by a bus on the way home, are you prepared to enter eternity?" (To this day I have a morbid fear of buses!) His words cut like a knife. I knew I was not ready. And later that night my father explained the good news about Christ in more detail.

I trusted Christ as my Savior right then and there, and from that moment on my eternal destiny was settled. I went from being a hell-bound sinner to being a heaven-bound Christian. I trusted Christ not so that I would have a better day tomorrow, but so that I was prepared to face eternity. I understood the simple principle that we are not promised tomorrow. "Come now, you who say, 'Today or tomorrow we will go to such and such a city, spend a year there, buy and sell, and make a profit;' whereas you do not know what will happen tomorrow. For what is your life? It is even a vapor that appears for a little time and then vanishes away" (James 4:13–14).

Jesus said that those who fail to believe in Him will "die in their sins" (John 8:24). This means that they will die without having remedied their sin problem by believing the Gospel, and thus will pay the ultimate consequence for their sin. Jesus describes this as *perishing*. "For God so loved the world that He gave His only begotten Son, that whoever believes in Him should not perish but have everlasting life" (John 3:16). *Perishing* is in contrast to *eternal life*.

As bad as sin's predicament is, God's provision is equal to the task!

Do you comprehend the full gravity of sin? To truly comprehend your sinfulness, you must acknowledge that sin has created a disconnection with God that has eternal ramifications. Acknowledging your sinfulness includes recognizing that sin separates you from God, which ultimately results in eternal damnation in hell (Gen 2:7; Rom 5:1–10; 6:23). But remember…as bad as sin's predicament is, God's provision is equal to the task! Christ died for our sins and rose from the dead.

So far we have seen that believing in Jesus for eternal life means recognizing that He is the Son of God who died and rose again to pay our sin debt and give us the free gift of eternal life. But there is one final yet equally indispensable component of the content of saving faith: the *exclusivity of faith in Jesus Christ*.

Jesus Is the Only Way to Eternal Life

By *exclusivity*, we mean that Jesus is the only way to eternal life. The path to eternal salvation is not a multiple choice quiz. It is not a matter of choosing one option among many equally valid ones. Simply put, you cannot be saved unless you have placed your faith in Jesus Christ, *and Him alone,* to save you.

Let's suppose a person recognizes his sin problem and decides that he needs to do something about it if he wants to have eternal life. And let's suppose he researches several options such as Islam, Buddhism, Christianity, and New Age. After looking them over, he decides that faith alone in Christ alone is the *best* option, but he concludes that *all of them* are valid pathways to heaven. This is not saving faith. Saving faith is exclusive faith.

Saving faith is exclusive faith.

You cannot believe Jesus is your only hope of eternal salvation while at the same time believing that other options exist. This is a logical fallacy. The gift of eternal life that Christ offers demands exclusive faith in Him. He said plainly, "I am the Way, the Truth, and the Life. No one comes to the Father *except by Me*" (John 14:6).

Consider the analogy of a key. Suppose you hold in your possession a key ring filled with dozens of different keys. Then suppose a man comes to you and asks for the key that will open a particular door—let's call it "Door A." You rifle through your keys and find the one and only key that opens Door A, and you give it to the man who made the request. Would you also then give him a second key that *does not* open Door A and say, "Here you go. Here are two keys. Use either one." That would be nonsensical. You know that *only one key works.*

Similarly, trusting Christ for eternal salvation, while at the same time believing that other pathways to heaven exist, is evidence that you do not understand Christ's offer of salvation. It shows a failure to comprehend everything we have been talking about. If other options exist, then Jesus is not the unique Son of

God. If other options exist, then Jesus' death and resurrection were unnecessary. If other options exist, then who really paid our sin debt? If other options exist, then what is so amazing about God's grace? And so on.

The path to eternal salvation is indeed free, but there is only one free ticket that will open the door of heaven—*faith in Christ.* The reason salvation is free to us is because the high cost of sin was paid for by our Savior. *No one else paid this price,* and thus no one else has the right or ability to offer us the free gift.

Saving faith is exclusive faith. If you believe that eternal life is gained by trusting Christ *and* doing good works; or by trusting Christ *and* being baptized, etc.; or if you believe that faith in Christ is just one of many valid pathways to eternal life, then your faith is not in the proper object and thus is not saving faith. Faith that does not rest solely on Jesus Christ as the only One who can pay your penalty for sin and give you the free gift of eternal life is not saving faith. Period.

It is clear that Jesus demands exclusivity by many statements He made in the Bible. But the Apostle Peter likewise affirms the exclusivity of faith in Christ for eternal salvation. In his famous address before the Sanhedrin, Peter declared, "Let it be known to you all, and to all the people of Israel, that by the name of Jesus Christ of Nazareth, whom you crucified, whom God raised from the dead, by Him this man stands here before you whole. This is the 'stone which was rejected by you builders, which has become the chief cornerstone.' Nor is there salvation in any other, for there is *no other name under heaven given among men by which we must be saved*" (Acts 4:10–12).

Similarly, the Apostle Paul leaves no room for alternate routes to eternal salvation. "For this is good and acceptable in the sight of God our Savior, who desires all men to be saved and to come to the knowledge of the truth. For there is one God and *one Mediator between God and men, the Man Christ Jesus,* who gave Himself a ransom for all, to be testified in due time" (1 Timothy 2:3–6).

Saving faith is faith in Christ *alone* for eternal life. Insisting on the exclusivity of Christ is especially important in light of the prevailing mindset of our culture. A contemporary confession of faith, referred to as the "Amsterdam Declaration, 2000: A Charter for Evangelism in the 21st Century," accurately captures the importance of proclaiming the exclusivity of Christ in a world where contradictory worldviews are increasingly embraced as equally valid. Part of the Amsterdam Declaration states:

> Today's evangelist is called to proclaim the gospel in an increasingly pluralistic world. In this global village of competing faiths and many world religions, it is important that our evangelism be marked both by faithfulness to the good news of Christ and humility in our delivery of it. Because God's general revelation extends to all points of his creation, there may well be traces of truth, beauty and goodness in many non-Christian belief systems. But we have no warrant for regarding any of these as alternative gospels or separate roads to salvation.

Indeed, there are no separate roads to salvation. There is only one road. The essence of saving faith is plain and simple: Jesus Christ, the Son of God, died and rose again to pay your sin debt. Only by trusting in Him, and Him alone, can you receive the free gift of eternal life.

So where does that leave us? We have seen that the Bible is our only Playbook. It is the only standard for our beliefs, attitudes and behaviors. We have seen that the Bible gives us a specific game plan to overcome our sin problem—the Gospel. We have seen that the Gospel involves our *predicament* (sin), God's *provision* (grace), and our *profession* (faith alone in Christ). We also examined precisely what we have to believe about Jesus in order to receive the free gift of eternal life.

All that remains is to see beyond the distractions of life that blind you to the Gospel and take care of what matters most. Are you ready? If so, read on. It is time to get serious about life. It is time to embrace the plain and simple good news of the Bible.

· · ·

Chapter Four Discussion Questions

1.   What is faith?

2.   What is saving faith?

3. Why is it important to identify the precise content of saving faith?

4. What precisely must a person believe about Jesus Christ to have eternal life?

5.   What do we mean when we say that *saving faith* is *exclusive faith*?

5

BELIEVE THE GOOD NEWS

"This one word 'believe' represents all a sinner
can do and *all a sinner must do to be saved.*"
(Lewis Sperry Chafer)

Christ died for our sins and rose from the dead. That really
is *good news*! Think about it. Without Christ's work on the cross,
we are all left dead in our tracks. We have no hope. We are utterly
helpless to overcome the penalty of sin without Him. Without
Christ we face an eternity in torment. Without Christ, we are
like strangers "having no hope and without God in the world"
(Eph 2:12).

But in Christ Jesus, those of us who were "once far off have
been brought near by the blood of Christ" (Eph 2:13). The
separation between us and God created by our sin is removed.
God's anger is satisfied. The penalty has been paid. What a
difference! And it all comes down to faith in Christ. *Know Christ.
Know peace. No Christ. No peace.* It really is as simple as that.
More than 200 times, the Bible conditions eternal life upon
faith alone in Christ alone.

How can we possibly
get something as
valuable as eternal
life for free?

You might be thinking that
this all sounds too good to be true.
Surely there must be something
that we have to do to gain eternal
life. How can we possibly get
something as valuable as eternal
life for free? The answer is found
within the question itself. Eternal

life is so valuable—it comes at such a high price—that there is only One person who can pay it: Jesus Christ. And having paid the price, He now offers it freely to all who will simply believe in Him for it. The invitation to accept the good news is clear in the Bible. "Whoever desires, let him take the water of life *freely*" (Revelation 22:17).

> **"To believe on Christ is to see and believe the all-sufficiency of His saving grace."**
> **(Lewis Sperry Chafer)**

The Bible predicts that many people will stumble over the simplicity of the Gospel. "For the message of the cross is foolishness to those who are perishing, but to us who are being saved it is the power of God" (1 Cor 1:18). Remember what we said earlier. The *Gospel* is the power of God to salvation to everyone who believes it (Rom 1:16). The Gospel is what matters most. Are you willing to look beyond all of the distractions of life and focus on the Gospel?

Bright Lights and Other Distractions

Teaching a fifteen year old how to drive poses a number of challenges. I speak from experience. I've done it twice, and I have four more coming behind them. (Please join me in praying for the imminent return of Christ. I'm not sure my heart can handle four more teenage drivers!)

In the first place, many of the skills we use for driving are instinctive or intuitive, and come with practice. For example, you cannot teach a first-time driver how to react when an empty bag of feed corn flies out of the back of a pick-up truck in front of you, and blows right into your path—obscuring your view for one, short terrifying moment. In the second place, since fifteen year olds already know everything, almost nothing that is said by their driving instructor will be welcomed and embraced. Teaching our children to drive is just another in a long list of the joys of parenting!

I recall one occasion when I was giving my oldest daughter some practice time behind the wheel. We approached a turn onto a major highway. As she (and I!) looked back to our left to look for oncoming traffic, the bright eastern sun blinded us and made it difficult to see if any cars were coming. It didn't help matters that our windows were coated in dust from our gravel driveway, causing the sun to reflect and create a shadow effect—further shielding our view.

Eventually, we were able to gain a degree of confidence that it was safe to enter the highway, and the experience turned into a teachable moment about bright lights and other driving distractions.

There are many distractions that easily rob our focus and shift our attention away from the things that matter most.

Life, like driving, comes down to focus. There are many distractions that easily rob our focus and shift our attention away from the things that matter most. Jesus calls such distractions the "cares of this world" that "choke the Word" in our lives and hinder our spiritual growth (Matt 13:22). It is axiomatic that our focus determines our direction: *You always hit what you are aiming for.*

For example, if your eyes shift to the scenery on your left, your hands on the steering wheel will follow and your car inevitably drifts across the yellow stripe and into the oncoming traffic. Any carpenter worth his salt knows that when hammering nails, you focus on the *nail* not your *thumb. You always hit what you are aiming at.*

The Bible cautions, "Wisdom is in the sight of him who has understanding, but the eyes of a fool are on the ends of the earth" (Prov 17:24). In other words, the eyes of a fool wander all over the place, but a discerning person keeps wisdom in view. Fools lack focus. And Satan takes advantage of this weakness by blinding the minds of unbelievers "lest the light of the gospel of the glory of Christ, who is the image of God, should shine on them" (2 Cor 4:4).

Those who are wise keep their eyes on the target. Where is your focus? Are you allowing bright lights and other distractions to divert you from what matters most? The Bible is a lamp to our feet and a light to our path (Ps 119:105). It is the right Playbook with the only winning game plan.

To believe the Gospel requires nothing more than confidence that what Jesus has promised is true.

To believe the Gospel requires nothing more than confidence that what Jesus has promised is true. Generically speaking, *faith* is assurance or confidence in the truth of some object. *Saving faith* occurs when faith meets the right object—the Gospel. Though there are many things that you can and do believe throughout your life, what matters most is whether or not you have believed in Jesus Christ, the Son of God, who died and rose again to pay your personal penalty for sin, as the only One who can give you eternal life.

Cloudy Medicine

Some time ago Wendy was dispensing a dropper full of medicine to our daughter Faith. While mom was administering the medicine, our son Landry, who was two years old at the time, grabbed the medicine bottle and tried to play pharmacist by pouring milk from his sippy cup into the open bottle. Before Wendy could get the bottle away from him a drop or two of milk had escaped from the sippy cup and landed right in the medicine bottle. As Wendy looked discouragingly at the cloudy medicine, she realized the entire bottle had to be thrown away. Even though the bottle contained 99% medicine and less than 1% milk, it was still contaminated and unfit for use.

It has been nearly 2000 years since Jesus died and rose again to pay the penalty for sin and provide eternal salvation to all who will simply receive it. Yet efforts to gain heaven on the merits of one's own righteous acts are still contaminating the pure message of grace. The pride of men and women is so strong that it will not allow them to believe that they can get something as valuable as forgiveness and eternal life for free. This is in spite of the fact that the Apostle Paul and the other early church leaders taught that the true gospel message was one of salvation by grace through faith as a *free gift* from God. Listen to what Paul said about the Jews in the first century: "For they being ignorant of God's righteousness, and *seeking to establish their own righteousness*, have not submitted to the righteousness of God" (Rom. 10:3).

> **The righteousness that God's holiness demands is perfect righteousness.**

What Paul was saying could not be clearer: The righteousness that God's holiness demands is perfect righteousness. If we could gain eternal life by keeping the law, Christ's death was irrelevant. Plus, anyone who hopes to justify himself before God by keeping the law must be willing to keep *all of it*. Since this is impossible, eternal salvation must come from some other source. There must be some other means by which we can gain perfect righteousness. There is. It's called *grace.*

At first this teaching may sound too good to be true. But that is what makes grace so amazing. You cannot earn it….it is free! That is the essence of grace. It is undeserved, unmerited favor. You can keep trying to earn heaven by your own righteous behavior if you want to. But just remember, righteousness gained by human effort is just cloudy medicine. The Bible says, "For whoever shall keep the whole law, and yet stumble in one point, he is guilty of all" (James 2:10).

In other words, no matter how much medicine is in the bottle, if you add even one ounce of human effort, it spoils the whole batch. When it comes to keeping the law, close does not count. Close may count in horseshoes and hand grenades, but not when it comes to what matters most—eternal salvation. If you want it, you must simply receive it. It is a gift. It cannot be earned.

Do you want to be sure of your eternal destiny? Jesus said to those who believe in Him, "I give them eternal life, and they shall never perish; neither shall anyone snatch them out of My hand" (John 10:28). Assurance is as simple as knowing whether or not you have believed the good news. You do not have to spend your life wondering where you will end up in eternity. You can know for sure. Now.

> "It is quite possible for any intelligent person to know whether he has placed such confidence in the Savior. Saving faith is a matter of personal consciousness. 'I know whom I have believed.' To have deposited one's eternal welfare in the hands of another is a decision of the mind so definite that it can hardly be confused with anything else. *On this deposit of oneself into His saving grace depends one's eternal destiny.*"
> (Lewis Sperry Chafer)

A Measure of Assurance?

Sadly however, many people go through life satisfied with only a measure of assurance. There is always a nagging doubt as they wonder whether or not Jesus really meant it when He promised eternal life to all who simply trust in Him. But partial assurance is no assurance at all. Allow me to illustrate the point.

My favorite kind of cookie is chocolate chip. There is scarcely anything better than a hot, just-out-of-the-oven, homemade chocolate chip cookie with a cold glass of milk. When I was a teenager, I used to make them myself, using Mom's family recipe. The first time I did, though, turned out to be quite a fiasco. You see, the recipe card was so old and tattered from years of use that some of the instructions were hard to read. In particular, the measurement amounts were difficult to discern.

When it came time to add the brown sugar, I thought it said "12 cups," when in reality it said, "1/2 cup." Big difference! A quick consultation with Mom clarified the matter, and needless to say that first batch of cookies was scrapped and the second batch came out much better.

There is a valuable lesson in this humorous experience: If you do not know the precise measurement a recipe calls for, the result can be disastrous. The same can be said of the believer's assurance. A growing number of Bible teachers and theologians today are suggesting that your assurance of eternal salvation is based upon "some measure" of good works, without specifying precisely how many good works are necessary to assure you that you are indeed saved.

One famous Bible teacher writes, "There is no doubt that Jesus saw some measure of real, lived-out obedience to the will of God as necessary for final salvation." Wow! Did you notice his reference to "some measure?" Think about that for a moment. If the determinative factor in our eternal salvation is "some measure of real, lived-out, obedience to the will of God," one understandably might want to know *how much* obedience? Do I need 12 cups of obedience? Or is it only ½ a cup of obedience? What exactly does he mean by "some measure?" It sounds conspicuously vague. How can I ever know if I have produced a "measure" of good works acceptable enough to get me into heaven?

Recall that the Bible is crystal clear that good works can never earn us entrance into heaven. It is only by grace. Why then, as this author suggests, would we want to look to our works for the assurance of our eternal destiny?

And this writer is not alone. Another well-known Bible teacher shares the same view. He suggests that for a person to get to heaven he must not only believe the Gospel, but he must produce good works. He writes, "True faith is always accompanied by non-saving, but absolutely necessary works… If there are no good works, there is no true faith." It is not unreasonable to ask how good works can be both "non-saving" but "absolutely necessary" at the same time. If good works are absolutely necessary for eternal salvation, as these two men suggest, then does that not make them *determinative* in our eternal salvation?

There is no quantifiable way to measure how many good works a person must perform in order to be assured that he is saved. If, as one of these Bible teachers states, "good works are absolutely necessary" as "proof" that one is a Christian, then how much proof is enough? What's the measure?

Contrary to the assertions of these men (and many others), our assurance of salvation is *not* based upon our good works. It is "not by works of righteousness which we have done, but according to His mercy that He saved us" (Titus 3:5). My assurance of eternal salvation is based solely upon the promise of Jesus Christ, My Savior, who says to those who trust in Him, "I give them eternal life, and they shall never perish; neither shall anyone snatch them out of My hand" (John 10:28). If Jesus meant what He said (and He did!), then my salvation is both sure and secure. I need look only to His promise for assurance. If I look at my works as the basis for assurance—trying

> My assurance of eternal salvation is based solely upon the promise of Jesus Christ, My Savior, who says to those who trust in Him, "I give them eternal life, and they shall never perish; neither shall anyone snatch them out of My hand."

to discover some ambiguous measure—I will doubt my salvation every day.

> "From the testimony of the Scriptures, a Christian should know that he is saved. There is abundant Biblical witness on this point, and it can hardly be deemed commendable to be in doubt on this vital question... If salvation depends in any degree on personal goodness, there could not be even a saved person in the world, and therefore no ground in it for assurance."
> (Lewis Sperry Chafer)

But if I go back to the source of my salvation to clarify the matter—Jesus Christ Himself—there can be no doubt. He said, "I give you eternal life and you will never perish." Even if I stumble; even if I fall sometimes; whether I have ½ a cup of good works or 12 cups of good works, I can be sure that my faith alone in Christ alone—the Son of God who died and rose again for my sins—has secured for me my eternal salvation. "For by grace are you saved through faith, and that not of yourselves, it is the gift of God. Not of works, lest any man should boast" (Ephesians 2:8–9). That's good news!

In the final analysis, if a "measure of good works" is necessary for eternal salvation, then the best we can ever hope for is a "measure of assurance." For me, that is not enough. I want to have absolute, 100% assurance of my salvation. What about you? Have you trusted in Jesus Christ and Him alone for eternal salvation? If so, then you can be sure you have eternal life and that it can never be lost again.

Eternal Means Eternal

It is amazing, though not surprising in this age where words no longer have inherent meaning, that some would suggest the gift of eternal life can somehow be taken away. Think about that for a moment. Forget all of the theological speculations you have heard. Set aside your presuppositions. Just think about the words *eternal life*. If the gift that God gives you the moment you trust in Jesus Christ is only temporary, or could somehow be lost again, why in the world would God call it *eternal*? Repeatedly. Over and over again. Throughout the Bible. It doesn't make any sense.

The fact is salvation cannot be lost.

The fact is salvation cannot be lost. Trusting Christ brings with it the free gift of *eternal* life, which by definition can never be lost. It is a present possession that begins at a moment of faith and never ends. Earlier, we listed several passages that emphasize the eternal nature of salvation. We demonstrated that according to the Bible, the consequence for sin is *eternal* torment and by contrast the result of receiving the free gift of salvation by faith in Christ is *eternal* life.

The truth that God's gift of eternal salvation can never be lost is what Bible scholars refer to as the doctrine of *eternal security*. The doctrine of eternal security states that a person who has obtained eternal life (i.e. has become a Christian by faith in Jesus Christ) cannot forfeit eternal life because of his actions. The Bible teaches that once a person is saved from hell, he is always saved. Nothing can cause his salvation to be taken away. Therefore, even if subsequent to becoming a Christian, someone commits sins—even grievous sins—he cannot lose his salvation. Since we are not saved by works, we cannot become *unsaved* by works.

The doctrine of eternal security is often confused with the doctrine of assurance. However the two doctrines are distinct. As we discussed in the previous section *assurance* refers to the fact that a Christian can know for certain (be *assured*) that he has eternal life. The doctrine of eternal security, on the other hand, states that once a person is saved he is always saved. All Christians have eternal security, but unfortunately not all Christians have assurance.

Because of the prevalent false teaching that good works are necessary to gain eternal life, many people spend their entire lives doubting their salvation. This is unfortunate, because it leads to a defeated and ineffective life as a Christian. But even though a person may doubt his salvation, the Bible teaches if he has in fact trusted in Jesus Christ and Him alone for salvation, He is eternally secure.

There are many Bible passages that prove the eternal security of the believer. For example, Ephesians 1:13-14 tells us that all Christians receive the Holy Spirit the moment they believe the gospel as a seal guaranteeing their salvation until the day they reach heaven. 2 Corinthians 1:21-22 tells us that all Christians receive the Holy Spirit the moment they believe as a pledge of God's intentions to finish what He started. In John 10:28-30, Jesus Himself reminds us that He knows those who are His and promises that they will never perish. Philippians 1:6 also reminds us that God always finishes what He starts.

Eternal salvation is a work of God. It is dependent upon the work of God and not the works of men (Rom. 5:12-21). Works are not a requirement for eternal salvation (Eph 2:8-9; Titus 3:5). As we pointed out earlier, eternal salvation cannot be earned (Matt 5:20; Rom 9:30-33). If works are not a requirement to *receive* eternal salvation, then how can they be a requirement to *keep* eternal salvation? Neither the absence of good works, nor the presence of bad deeds, can affect your eternal salvation after you have received it as a free gift by faith alone.

> "The Gospel does not inspire a hope that God will be gracious: it discloses the good news that He has been gracious and challenges every man but to *believe* it. A criminal pleading for mercy before a judge is not in the same position as a criminal believing and rejoicing in the assurance that a full pardon is granted and that *he can never be brought again into judgment.*"
> (Lewis Sperry Chafer)

Remember what we said about justification? Justification is a legal term that means to be "declared righteous." In its original use, the Greek term referred to a legal act of charging something to someone's account. In the context of salvation, it refers to the act of God whereupon He declares that a sinful person has been credited with the perfect righteousness of Jesus Christ. This justification by God occurs at the moment we believe the gospel (Rom 4:5; 5:1; 10:4).

The moment a person believes the Gospel, God—the omnipotent Judge—declares him to be once and for all innocent and completely righteous. The verdict is in. The gavel has landed. Court is adjourned. To say that someone could become unsaved after being saved would be to say that God changed His mind or reneged on His ruling. It would also make the Gospel out to be only *potential* good news, not *actual* good news. Indeed, it is not good news at all to say to someone that they can have the free gift of eternal life, but they better watch out because if they slip up it can be taken away.

Eternal salvation is based on the promise of Christ who said of believers "I give them eternal life and they shall never perish (John 10:28)." Jesus stakes His promise of eternal life upon His Father's word when He says that no one can snatch us out of His Father's hand (John 10:29). God's very word is at stake and God cannot lie (Titus 1:2).

The moment a person believes the Gospel, he is adopted into the family of God (Rom 8:15-17; Gal 4:4-5). He becomes a child of God (1 John 3:1). To say that eternal salvation can be lost is to speak of disowning a member of the family. If such were the case then the adoption of believers into the family of God is not permanent and the endearing term "child of God" is inaccurate. It would be nothing more than a hollow label devoid of any significance.

The bottom line is....eternal means eternal. That's good news, plain and simple.

> **My hope is built on nothing less**
> **Than Jesus' blood and righteousness;**
> **I dare not trust the sweetest frame,**
> **But wholly lean on Jesus' Name.**
> **On Christ, the solid Rock, I stand;**
> **All other ground is sinking sand.**

One Final Challenge

With so much uncertainty in the world today, it is great to know there is something we can really count on. The Gospel. It is good news, plain and simple. But as plain and simple as it is, the Gospel does not force itself upon anyone. Like any gift, it must be received before its benefits can be enjoyed.

You've heard the evidence straight from the Playbook—The Bible. It is clear. You've examined the game plan—The Gospel. It is plain and simple. You know the predicament you face—Sin and its eternal consequence. It is a serious issue that must be dealt with. You know precisely what you have to believe in order to receive forgiveness of sins and eternal life. Jesus Christ is the Son of God who died and rose again for your sins. And you understand that there is no other way to solve your

> Is there anything keeping you right now, this moment, from trusting in Jesus Christ for eternal life?

sin problem. Jesus is the only way to eternal life.

Only one question remains. Is there anything keeping you right now, this moment, from trusting in Jesus Christ for eternal life?

. . .

Chapter Five Discussion Questions

1. What one word is used more than 200 times in the Bible to describe the only way for us to receive eternal life?

2. Why do you think so many people struggle with the simplicity of the Gospel message?

3. Is it possible for us to know for sure whether or not we have eternal life?

4. Once you have received the free gift of eternal life by believing the good news, can you ever lose it?

5.   Have you personally trusted in Jesus Christ and Him alone for the free gift of eternal life?

AFTERWORD

Good news—plain and simple. My prayer for everyone who reads this little book is that you are able to see just how plain and simple God's good news really is. Over the last 2,000 years, with a little help from the devil, we have done a pretty good job of taking something so simple and making it very complicated. Theologians like to do that sometimes, don't they?

The devil's goal is to keep the lost, lost; and to keep those who are saved, defeated. A twisted and distorted Gospel message accomplishes both tasks. It keeps the lost, lost because as we said earlier only an accurate Gospel message can result in salvation when believed. But an erroneous Gospel message also keeps the saved defeated because it makes us spend our life doubting and wondering whether or not we are really saved.

Hopefully this book stripped away all of the confusion and complexity and gave you a clear look at God's amazing story of redemption. If after reading this book you trusted Christ for your eternal salvation, would you do me a favor? I would love to hear from you. The best way to reach me is through my web site at www.notbyworks.org or you may email me at info@notbyworks.org. Drop me a line and let me know you have trusted Christ.

For those of you who already had trusted Christ prior to reading this book, let me encourage you to spread the good news about Christ. You should be so familiar with the Gospel that you should be able to share the essence of it and what it means to believe it in thirty seconds or less. It should roll off of your lips. Perhaps this book helped you gain a clearer understanding of God's good news.

Let your light so shine before others that they will see your good works and give glory to God. Practice "show and tell" evangelism. Show them you are different and then tell them why. It's all because of the Gospel!

Finally, perhaps you know someone who is unsaved and would benefit from this presentation of the Gospel. Please pass it on. If I can ever be of assistance, please contact me at <u>info@notbyworks.org</u>.

J.B.H.

FOR FURTHER STUDY

Anderson, David R. *Free Grace Soteriology*. Longwood, FL: Xulon Press, 2010.

Bing, Charles C. *Simply By Grace*. Grand Rapids: Kregel, 2009.

Chafer, Lewis Sperry. *Salvation*. New York: C. C. Cook, 1917.

Chafer, Lewis Sperry. *Systematic Theology. Vol. 3 Soteriology*. 8 vols. Dallas: Dallas Seminary Press, 1948.

Chafer, Lewis Sperry. *True Evangelism*. New York: Gospel Publishing House, 1911.

Hixson, J.B. *Getting the Gospel Wrong: The Evangelical Crisis No One Is Talking About*. Longwood, Fl: Xulon Press, 2008.

Ironside, Harry A. *God's Unspeakable Gift*. London: Pickering & Inglis, 1908.

Lightner, Robert Paul. *Sin, the Savior, and Salvation: The Theology of Everlasting Life*. Nashville: T. Nelson Publishers, 1991.

Martuneac, Lou. *In Defense of the Gospel*. Longwood, FL: Xulon Press, 2010.

Ryrie, Charles Caldwell. *So Great Salvation: What It Means to Believe in Jesus Christ*. Wheaton: Victor Books, 1989.

Ryrie, Charles C. *The Grace of God*. Chicago: Moody Press, 1963.

Stegall, Thomas L. *The Gospel of the Christ*. Milwaukee: Grace Gospel Press, 2009.

CPSIA information can be obtained at www.ICGtesting.com
234233LV00001B/2/P

9 781935 909125